SHEEP ON THE FARM

Joanne Mattern

D1303698

ROURKE PUBLISHING
www.rourkepublishing.com

www.rourkepublishing.com

PHOTO CREDITS: Title Page: © Lena Andersson; Page 3: © Michel de Nijsl; Page 5: © Lisa Quarfoth; Page 7: © Eric Gevaert; Page 8: © Vera Tomankova; Page 9: © Tyler Olson; Page 10: © Marilyn Barbone; Page 11: © Ruth Black; Page 13: © Roman Milert; Page 14: © Rebecca Romano; Page 15: © Dennis Steen; Page 17: © Geoff Kuchera; Page 18: © sabrina dei nobili; Page 19: © Lutz Kupferschläger; Page 20: © Nicole S. Young; Page 21: © esemelwe; Page 22: Pete Saloutos; Back Ground: © Michael Fernhal

Edited by Precious McKenzie

Cover by Nicola Stratford, Blue Door Publishing
Interior design by Tara Raymo

Library of Congress Cataloging-in-Publication Data

Mattern, Joanne, 1963-
 Sheep on the farm / Joanne Mattern.
     p. cm. -- (On the farm)
 Includes bibliographical references and index.
 ISBN 978-1-61590-267-5 (Hard Cover) (alk. paper)
 ISBN 978-1-61590-507-2 (Soft Cover)
 1. Sheep--Juvenile literature. 2. Sheep ranches--Juvenile literature. I. Title.
 SF375.2.M38 2011
 636.3--dc22
                                    2010009855

Rourke Publishing
Printed in the United States of America, North Mankato, Minnesota
033010
033010LP

www.rourkepublishing.com - rourke@rourkepublishing.com
Post Office Box 643328 Vero Beach, Florida 32964

Table of Contents

Where Sheep Live

Sheep live on farms all around the world. You will find sheep in many different countries. Many sheep live on farms in the United States.

A sheep's wool coat keeps it warm even on a cold day.

Sheep Facts

Sheep are **mammals**. A female sheep, or **ewe**, weighs between 100 and 225 pounds (45 and 102 kilograms).

Sheep have a special stomach that helps them digest grass.

A male sheep is a **ram**. A ram weighs up to 350 pounds (159 kilograms).

Lambs drink milk from their mothers.

Most **lambs** are born in the spring.

Usually, a ewe gives birth to one lamb.

Sometimes, a ewe will have twins!

Lambs can walk soon after they are born.

Eating and Sleeping

Sheep eat grass and other plants like clover. You may see a **flock**, or group, of sheep grazing on the plants growing in a field. Sheep spend about seven hours grazing each day. Now that's a long lunch!

For protection, sheep stay close to other members of their flock.

Sheep often sleep outside, even in cold weather.

Sheep spend most of their days outside. At night, they might sleep in the barn. In warm weather, the sheep might sleep outside.

Sheep can sleep standing up or lying down.

Life on the Farm

A farmer takes good care of the sheep. The sheep eat grass on the farm. Special dogs **herd** the sheep. They also keep the sheep safe from **predators** like wolves, coyotes, eagles, and wild cats.

Just one or two dogs can herd and protect a large flock of sheep.

How Sheep Help People

Sheep help people in many ways. We eat their meat. We also use their milk to make cheese.

How To Make Cheese

Step 1: Cheese makers separate the cheese curds from the whey.

Step 2: Cheese makers salt and then shape the cheese curd.

Step 3: The cheese is set on shelves to age and to dry.

Products, such as cheese, made from sheeps milk feed people all over the world.

A farmer **shears** off the sheep's **wool** coat in the spring. People use the sheep's wool **fleece** to make clothes.

Shearing a sheep is like giving the sheep a haircut. It doesn't hurt them!

Sheep make a farm a fun place to live!

Glossary

ewe (YOO): a female sheep

fleece (FLEESS): a sheep's coat

flock (FLOK): a group of sheep

herd (HURD): to make animals move together as
a group

lambs (LAMZ): baby sheep

mammals (MAM-uhlz): warm-blooded animals that
have backbones

predators (PRED-uh-turz): animals that eat other animals

ram (RAM): a male sheep

shears (SHEERZ): cuts

wool (WUL): the soft, thick, curly hair of a sheep

Index

Websites to Visit

www.kiddyhouse.com/Farm/Sheep/sheep.html

www.kidsfarm.com/sheep.htm

www.enchantedlearning.com/subjects/mammals/farm/
Sheepprintout.shtml

About the Author

Joanne Mattern has written more than 300 books. She lives in New York State with her husband, four children, and an assortment of pets that includes cats, geckos, fish, and a turtle, but no sheep.